TO MY DAUGHTERS, never stop pursuing your dreams.

TO MY HUSBAND, thank you for your assistance.

ENRICO FABRIZI, thanks for your help, support, and encouragement with the Faith, Hope, and Love books and with my business venture. You continue to make a great impact on people's lives and build and grow great teams and leaders through your encouragement, listening, and support. Thanks for your leadership and support in these projects and in my journey.

RICHARD PAUL LILLY, thank you for all of your assistance with the illustrations for *Cast Your Cares* and *Happy in Hope*. Your creativity throughout really displayed itself in the projects. I appreciate you sharing your thoughts and ideas for the illustrations and your artistic ability. The illustrations are beautifully done.

Finally, I am thankful to the Lord for the words on the page and the encouragement those words have brought to people.

May the God of hope fill you with all joy and peace as you trust in Him, so that you may overflow with hope by the power of the Holy Spirit.

- *Romans 15:13*

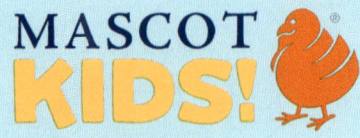

www.mascotbooks.com

Happy in Hope

©2021 Kristina Gipe. All Rights Reserved. No part of this publication may be reproduced, stored in a retrieval system or transmitted in any form by any means electronic, mechanical, or photocopying, recording or otherwise without the permission of the author.

For more information, please contact:
Mascot Books
620 Herndon Parkway, Suite 320
Herndon, VA 20170
info@mascotbooks.com

Library of Congress Control Number: 2021906327

CPSIA Code: PRT0821A
ISBN-13: 978-1-68401-907-6

Printed in the United States

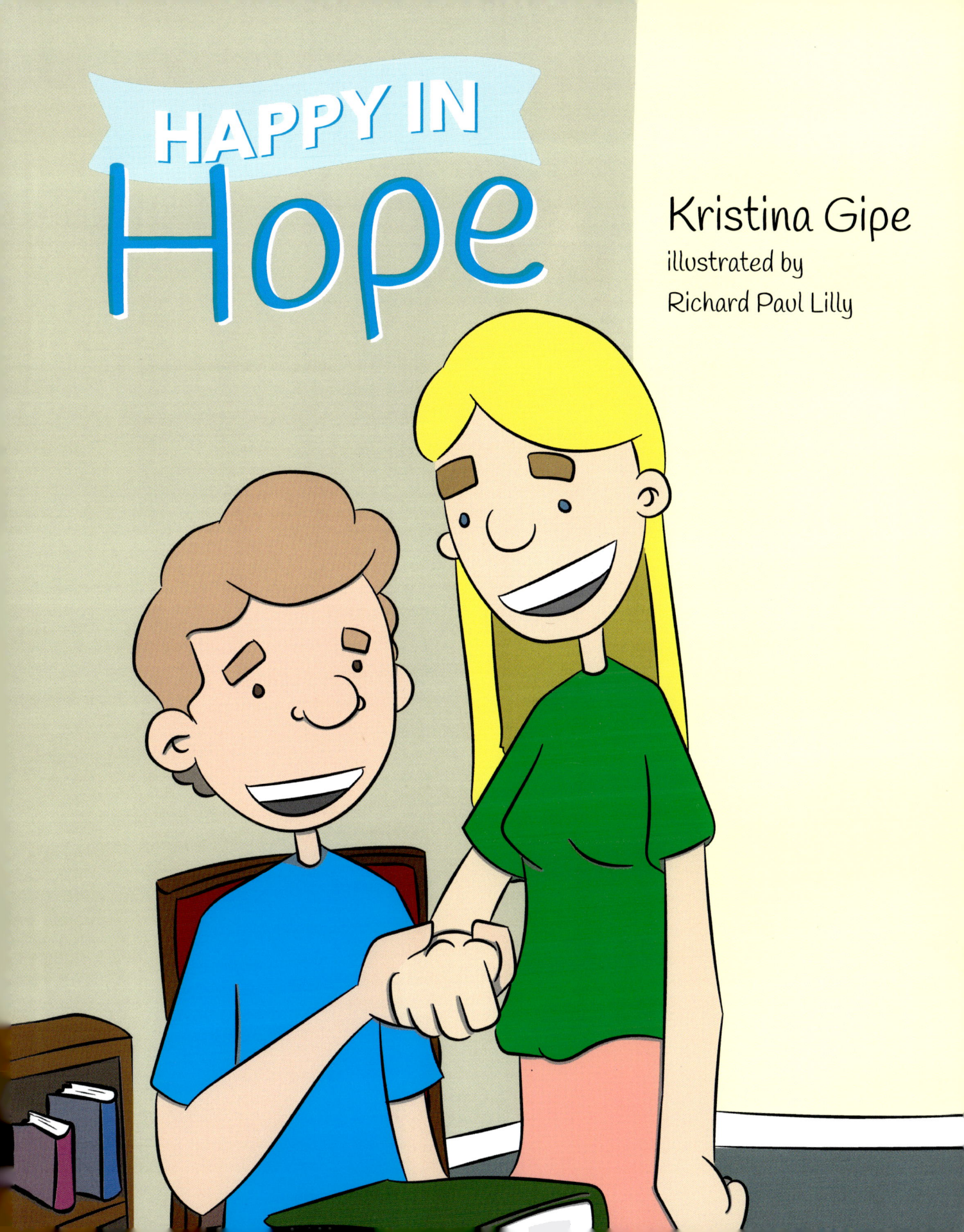

His Word guides us in our life,
providing strength for our soul when we face strife.

Trusting in the guidance of His Word and that it will provide the way
will fill our hearts and minds with peace and joy as we seek Him each day.

WE CAN TALK TO GOD knowing he hears our prayer, and for us will always be there.

The joy brought through the Lord can give us great rest, knowing He knows for us what is best.

Speaking to Him through our prayers will help lessen our cares.

THROUGH HOPE, joy fills our hearts and minds,
knowing that our relationship with God is the greatest one we'll find.

He gives us His peace each day
through taking time to be with Him and pray.

Some days might make us sad, but knowing He's in control can make our hearts and minds be glad.

God's Word can provide direction for each day,
as we read through it and pray.

When things in our lives turn out different than we thought they would,
placing hope in God helps us know in our hearts that things will work out as they should.

HOPE can help restore peace and joy to us each day, through placing our cares in God's hands, knowing He knows the way.

When we see things around us that may make us have fear, placing our hope in God says the Lord will make all things right and is always near.

God sees all things from above,
and He stretches out to the world His arms that are full of love.

Hope says, "God, I trust you with my mind and heart,
and know that you are a light when the path is unknown and dark."

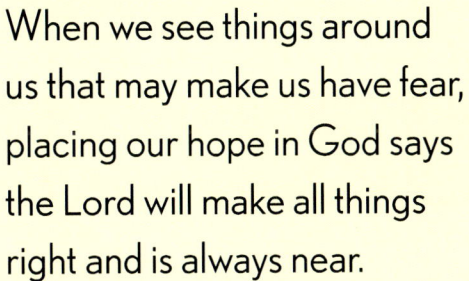

ALL OUR DAYS He will carry us through,
and each day we can stand in awe of what God can do.

Lifting the burdens of our heart to Him each day,
will help us stay on the right course and not lose our way.

He cares for everyone and listens as a loving friend to that which we have need.
He will see us through everything, and we can follow Him and His lead.

By having God's Word as an anchor for our soul,
we will know what's right to do and can learn which way we should go.

HE WILL HELP US through when times are bad.
If we keep His Word close to our heart, it can give us hope and make us glad.

Trust allows us to know He's in control,
knowing the way of the truth is how I should go.

The calmness that God brings grants us joy and peace,
allowing fear and anxiety in our lives to cease.

His love is key in our life for all that we do,
for it makes each day exciting and new.

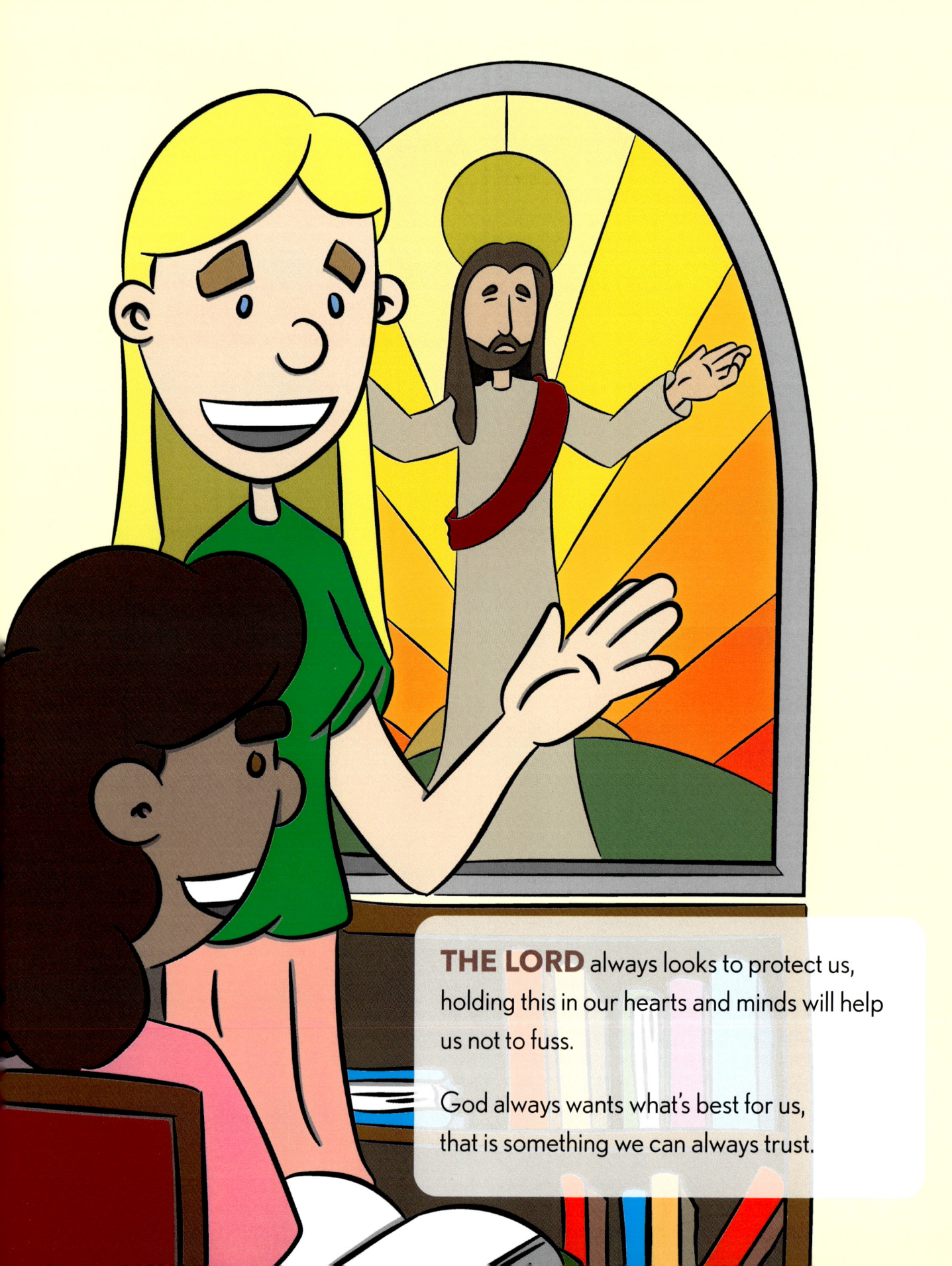

THE LORD always looks to protect us, holding this in our hearts and minds will help us not to fuss.

God always wants what's best for us, that is something we can always trust.

Through hope we surround ourselves in the Lord's love.
Knowing that we are in God's care as He watches our lives from Heaven above.

The Lord can calm our anxious soul.
We can rest easy knowing He's in control.

A SMILE can be brought to our face each day, when we take time to be with Him and pray.

When things at first don't go our way, Hope says, "I'll try again someday."

His desire for us is to succeed,
we just need to allow Him to lead.

God sent the Holy Spirit from above
to fill our hearts and minds with His truth and love.

God desires that no one be lost,
we hold in our hearts the hope of eternal life
through trusting in what Jesus Christ did on the cross.

WE CAN HOLD THE HOPE of eternity in
Heaven in our heart,
and know that through Jesus,
He's given us a fresh start.

God provides us hope for what each day may bring.
To Him we can give praise and sing.

His love so greatly surrounds us, bringing our hearts peace and joy from God above,
allowing us to turn away from Sin and closer each day to Him experiencing His love.

FAITH, HOPE, AND LOVE are wonderful things to hold on to,
knowing that every day of our lives God is with us and will help see us through.

We can have the hope of Heaven and great joy in our hearts and minds each day,
through placing our faith in Jesus' great love and His death on the cross being the way.

Knowing that His Word guides our way,
and that Jesus will return again someday.

ABOUT THE AUTHOR

Kristina Gipe received her Bachelor's Degree in Business, Management, and Economics with a concentration in Business Administration from Empire State College. The Lord placed it on her heart to write her first book *15 Days of Love*, where she began her journey and found an undiscovered passion for writing. The Lord inspires Kristina every day to grow in Faith, Hope, and Love.

ABOUT THE ILLUSTRATOR

Paul is an illustrator and graphic artist who considers himself a professional amateur. Practicing art both formally and informally since a young age, Paul has only recently started having work published. Besides this book, Paul has illustrated another published book as well as two graphic posters. Paul lives in Syracuse, New York, with his wife and two children.

OTHER BOOKS BY KRISTINA GIPE:

15 Days of Love

Cast Your Cares